BEING ME

For Jem, my lovely, funny, kind son – LB

Dedicated to the memory of Scott Hutchison (1981-2018),
and the work being done by 'Tiny Changes' –
a charity helping young minds feel better – MG

For Genevieve, Hector, Florence and Finnick – LM

Text copyright © Liz Brownlee, Matt Goodfellow, Laura Mucha 2021 except
Dropping the Ball copyright © Rochelle Burgess and Laura Mucha 2021,
The Land of Blue copyright © Laura Mucha 2017 (*A Poem for Every Day
of the Year*, ed Allie Esiri, Macmillan Children's Books)
Bottled Up © Laura Mucha 2019 (*Poems about Emotions*, Wayland)
Illustrations copyright © Victoria Jane Wheeler 2021

First published in Great Britain and in the USA in 2021 by
Otter-Barry Books, Little Orchard, Burley Gate, Herefordshire, HR1 3QS
www.otterbarrybooks.com

ISBN 978-1-91307-465-4

Illustrated with line drawings
Set in Avenir Book

Printed in Great Britain

9 8 7 6 5 4 3

BEING ME

Poems about Thoughts, Worries and Feelings

Poems by
Liz Brownlee
Matt Goodfellow
Laura Mucha

Illustrations by
Victoria Jane Wheeler

Otter-Barry BOOKS

Contents

Thought Machine

Sometimes my thought machine makes thoughts like

THAT WENT WELL or YOU'RE DOING GREAT or
YOU'VE GOT THIS

but sometimes it makes thoughts like

THAT WAS TERRIBLE or HOW EMBARRASSING or
WHAT A MESS

When that happens, I dance. Write. Run. Sing.
Listen to music. Talk. Swim.
I think of ONE thing I like about myself

NICE EARLOBES or GREAT DANCING or EXCELLENT
JOKES

and I set about my day.
And somehow, that pesky little thought machine
tends to think more positive things, like

THIS IS GOING WELL, YOU'RE DOING GREAT –
YOU'VE GOT THIS!

And I have.

Laura

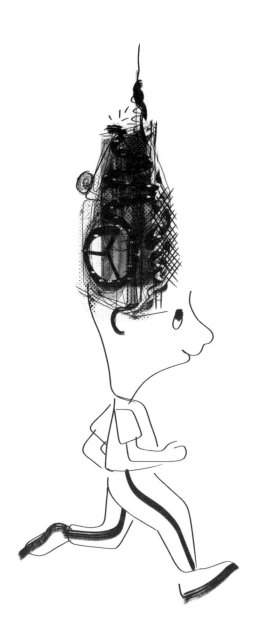

Back to Me

after
breakfast club
assembly
lessons
lunch
bell at three
care club
swimming
bus back home
I need a little
time alone
to just chill out
before my tea
and settle back
to being me

Matt

Kindness

It weighs as much as sound and light
and can be carried day and night

its trade is magic – dig down deep
for you'll still have as much to keep

and where you give it grows and grows
until one day it overflows

Liz

The Land of Blue

Across the valley it waits for you,
a place they call The Land of Blue.

It's far and near, it's strange yet known –
and in this land you'll feel alone,
you might feel tears roll down your cheek,
you might feel wobbly, weary, weak.

I know this won't sound fun to you –
it's not – this is The Land of Blue.
It's blue – not gold or tangerine,
it's dark – not light, not bright or clean.

It's blue – and when you leave, you'll see
the crackly branches of the tree,
the golden skies, the purring cat,
the piercing eyes, the feathered hat

and all the other things that come
when you escape from feeling glum.

Across the valley it waits for you,
a place they call The Land of Blue
and going there will help you know
how others feel when they feel low.

Laura

Secrets

The secret of the lightning
its electric, thundered spark
the secret of the stars' paths
that circle skies at dark
the secret of the stardust
that makes us and everything
the secret of the messages
that birds sing in the spring
the secrets of the universe
what made the world and how
these secrets are all ours to find
in the past, the future, now.

But the secrets kept within us
are more difficult to chart
given, or thrust upon us
those that please or crush the heart
no secret should be kept by threat
a burden to withhold
no secret should be kept for long –
there's none that can't be told.

Liz

Michael

Michael fell asleep in class last week,
face down on the desk.
Spark out in the middle of maths.
Mr Jones told us off for laughing, but
didn't seem cross with him at all.

Michael plays alone at break.
He just stands, staring into space,
watching the sky. Looking odd.
But the teacher on duty always goes
over and chats to him.
They never do that for us.

Michael only has a biscuit in his lunchbox
most days so the cook gives him stuff
for free.

Michael never takes his shoes and socks off
even when we do gym or dance
and Mr Jones lets him –
we all have to do it barefoot.

Michael gets loads of stickers
and certificates off all the adults
whenever he does anything.

Once, Leah swears she saw the Head,
Mrs Malone, wipe away a tear after she'd
seen his book and he'd only written a sentence.

Michael must be really lucky.

Matt

Free

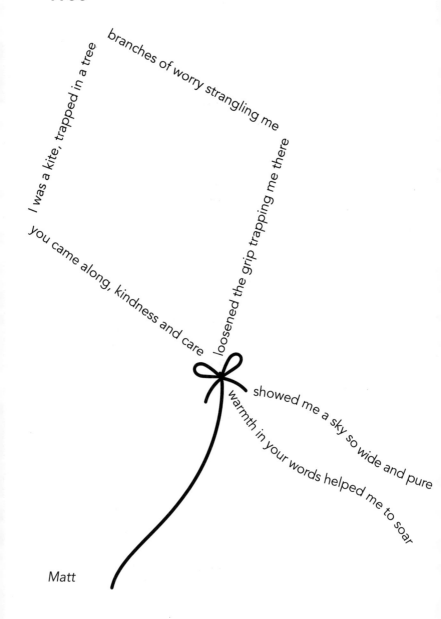

I was a kite, trapped in a tree

branches of worry strangling me

loosened the grip trapping me there

you came along, kindness and care

showed me a sky so wide and pure

warmth in your words helped me to soar

Matt

Chatting to my Inner Critic

I can.

You can't.

I can.

You can't.

Who says?

I do.

What do you know?

Everything.

No one knows everything.

I do.

No you don't.

I do.

I can.

You can't.

I can and I know what you're going to say...

You can't.

But I'm just going to let you say it...

You can't.

And ignore you.

You can't.

I'm not listening.

You can't.

I can.

You can't.

And I will.

You can't.

Because I can do anything.

Laura

Find Me

What makes me *me*
is on my mind

a place to fit
is hard to find

am I unique?
one of a kind?

I'm not the
same as them.

They know they are
just what they think

identity is
quite distinct

my puzzle piece
does not have links

I'm not the
same as them.

They don't know
I feel this way

I think of it
sometimes all day

I wonder if
it's safe to say

I'm not the
same as them.

Liz

A Thought

I wish Mum's sadness
was a necklace
she could unclasp
from her throat
in the cool bedroom-dark
and drop carelessly
into a mirrored box

in the morning
she'd throw back the curtains
open the box
see her sadness
and say

I choose not
to need
to wear you
today

Matt

I'm an Orchestra

Today I am the double bass,
solid, sonorous, strong.
I'm going somewhere, things to do,
always driving on.

But sometimes I'm the cor anglais,
solitary, subdued.
If my tone is wistful,
it's my melancholy mood.

Sometimes I'm the trumpet,
a spicy, strident sound,
and others the euphonium,
velvety and round.

I'm the triangle, worth the wait,
I'm the chimes, I captivate,
I'm the cymbals, clang and crash,
I'm a bass drum, meet your match,
I'm crotales, decisive, sure,
I'm the tam-tam.
              Hear.   My.   Roar.

I'm an orchestra.

Laura

Forest Song

there is music in the forest
every leaf a different note
as the wind-conducted branches
play the tune the raindrops wrote

so, go walk beneath the canopy
and know that you belong
to the purest ancient melody
as forest sings its song

Matt

The Nightingale

Hidden in the heart of darkling leaves he calls, notes flow in rivers and rapids and falls - he doesn't care for being the same as all the other birds, with their repeating calls - he sings to the sky at night. Sings alone. The loveliest song of them all

Liz

Read from left to right, from top to bottom

The Lump

They think if they don't talk, it won't happen.
They think if they don't talk, I won't notice.
They think if they don't talk, I won't feel sad.

But it's happening.
I've noticed.
And silence makes the sadness worse.

Laura

Can't Explain

my head my hands my face are fire
fast-blood veins electric wire
smash the classroom table chair
pixelated playground stare
still you ask what's in my brain
I'm eight years old
I can't explain

I can't explain how deep the hole
glass-lined static stabs my soul
how when it drains my bones are cold
I've done bad things again I'm told
angry eyes that call my name
I'm eight years old
I can't explain

Matt

My Head is Full of Hurry

so I find a patch of green
and sit.

Busy birds twitter and chunter,
chit-chattering about their day.
Flies lurk, loiter and listen,
wings shimmering till they whizz away.

Bees hum, bumble and mutter,
leaves flit, float and flutter,
and a squirrel comes out to play.

Butterflies flock in an elegant flurry,
dogs in a bustle scoot, scuttle and scurry,
and amid the hustle and rustle of the glade,
my mind's hurry   f
l
i
t
t
e
r
s

a
w
a
y.

Laura

The Thinking Tree

I've climbed right up to the top of this tree
just swaying branches, leaves and me

to spend a tiny bit of time
thinking thoughts inside my mind

like: what are we having for tea tonight?
I wish I could fly at the speed of light

why's there a 'k' at the start of 'knee'?
will I have a moustache when I'm 83?

why did Mum fall out with Dad –
and will he always look so sad?

if God is real, why so much pain?
has anyone prayed for flavoured rain?

when does sky turn into space?
what's the longest ever strawberry lace?

I'm hot I'm cold I'm turning green
I'm a choo-choo train with Marmite steam

a thousand thoughts all spinning round
so high above the distant ground

but the clearest thought up in this tree:
I think I'm stuck – and I need a wee

Matt

What to Do With Worries

Shout them to the ocean

sigh them to the moon

sing them to the sun

paint them in a picture

put them in a poem

chant them on a run

list them in a letter

post them in a box

solve them one by one

Liz

Arguing

they aren't
angry with me
they say

I am no
part of it

but they are
part of me
part of me
is each of them

and every time
their voices slam
and scream
mean words

they hurt a part
of who
I am

Liz

Bobby

Bobby **BOUNCES** off walls,

STOMPS

SHOUTS and

SMASHES.

He grabs my coat,

my skirt, my h

a

i

r

and SMIRKS.

He **JEERS** at teachers,

"This lesson is boring, Miss!"

"Do you have a boyfriend, Miss?"

"Why do I have to come to school anyway, Miss?"

SMACKS objects,

and **SCARES** students.

He doesn't care.

Bobby   steals rulers   and pencils   and   hope.

   He rules the corridor,

                  the classroom,

                           the school.

Nobody   nowhere   scares Bobby.

   He's not afraid of anything,   anywhere,   anyone.

      It's easy – you see,

               if others are frightened,

                        he doesn't have to be.

Laura

Bottled Up

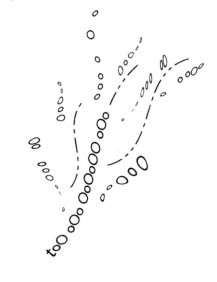

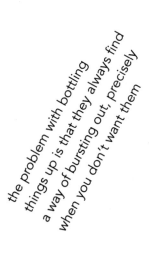

the problem with bottling
things up is that they always find
a way of bursting out, precisely
when you don't want them

Laura

A Pencil Speaks

I'm tired of this writing on paper
the wearing away of my lead

I'm fed up with their greasy fingers
and sharp teeth biting my head

I imagine a life that's exciting
to be more than just black on white

how I long to decide my own story
instead of what they want to write

I want to shout things that I shouldn't
to dance on my white paper floor

I won't keep in line and stay wooden
because that's what a pencil is for

I've decided to change my direction
I'm running away with my chum

he's going to train as a chopstick
and I'm going to learn to play drums.

Liz

Quiet Voices

the world is such

a noisy place

so many voices

spouting

shouting

for me

it's the quiet voices that rise above:

speaking kindness

speaking love

Matt

The Quiet Child

I am the person who listens
as people around me all talk

when everyone else is running
I notice each thing while I walk

I'll be the voice that questions
the accepted answers they gave

I am the leaf that trembles
while all the other leaves wave

as I have doubted the wind
and sensed that something is wrong

I am the one that's uncertain –
that is what makes me so strong

Liz

Dropping the Ball

Did I hear that right?

I couldn't have.

Mum said it might happen one day –

I must have got it wrong.

I thought he was my friend.

I thought he was kind.

My face is hot.

Everyone's looking now.

But black people don't blush so

Maybe no one will notice.

I'll pretend I'm fine.

She's being so brave.

I know, I'll get the ball.

Should I say something?

I can't. I can't move.

Should I give her a hug?

(Did he even say it?)

I don't know.

"Stupid monkey."

I know, I'll get the ball.

My hands are shaking.

And hold her hand.

Oh! Maybe I'm not so

So she doesn't feel so

alone.

Rochelle Burgess and Laura Mucha

One of These Days

I was born far away from the place I should be

in a cloud-covered town by a cold iron sea

where an oil-slick of boredom chokes everything

through holes in dead phone-boxes biting winds sing

but sometimes at night on the treacly tide

white lights of freedom call me to dive

into black water to shed this old skin

and one of these days I swear that I'll swim

Matt

Snail

I wish I had a home on my back – then I wouldn't move so often, then I wouldn't need new friends, then I would be safe.

Laura

Mrs Simon Said

there's a line across the classroom
invisible but there
a silent bind, a tether
from my table to your chair
that stops you drifting out
into the thoughtlessness of air

there's a line across the classroom
though the class are unaware
busy triviality
allows no time to spare
for seeing such a burden
but I notice
and I care

Matt

Promise

Consider the bulb:
no life to show
tangles of withered
roots below

dried husks surround
its bulbous form
it looks quite dead
but will transform

after the winter's
barren freeze
from earth to air
with unclasped leaves

its petals sunwrap
golden frills
its trumpet calls
in daffodil

the outer skin
just will not guide
the knowledge
of what hides inside

Liz

Differently Wired

you're algebra, you're long division

you're an added phrase that aids precision

you're improper fractions, column addition

you're apostrophes placed to show omission

you're a translated shape and its perfect reflection

you're i before e and every exception

there's nothing about you
that I understood

yet each of us knew
we'd found something good

someone to talk to
help us to heal

differently wired
friendship for real

Matt

I Believe in Me

I tore up the labels
that say what I am,
not a tick in a box,
a draft not a plan –

so sometimes I fail.
I don't need to be
as brilliant as them,
just be the best me.

I'm not what I do,
I'm not what you think;
I'm perfect but flawed,
I'm in pencil, not ink.

I believe in me.
One day I'll show them
that now I am just
an unedited poem.

Liz

Albatross

If I were an albatross,
I would share my anger with the wind,
drop my sadness into the depths of the valleys
and let my emptiness float above the trees.

If I were an albatross,
I would let my worries slip from the tips of my wings,
leave my loneliness to slide from the curve of my beak
and wonder at the wild of the water below.

If I were an albatross,
I would soar above the Antarctic sea
and leave all the mess of moving home, moving school,
and Dad leaving, behind me.

Laura

If Only

If only they'd told me that Granny would die,
I would have asked her questions, like:
   What should I be when I grow up?
   Are you proud of me?
   Where are you going?
I would have said:
   Is it my fault?
   Can I make you better?
   Will I catch it?
I would have whispered:
   Are you scared?
   Will you miss me?
   Will I be OK?

If only they'd told me that Granny would die,
I would have asked her all these questions.
   I would have said goodbye.

Laura

Today

today is a grey day
a don't-want-to-play day
a please-go-away day
they come now and then

a what's-it-about? day
a scream-and-a-shout day
a just-stick-it-out day
today's not my friend

Matt

In Betweens

Sometimes I fall in between
the cracks in the pavement
the faults in the system
the spaces in my dreams
the light through my fingers
the switching of the bulb
the good news, the bad news
the blanks between words
the lulls in the arguments

the gaps between us

Liz

Doing Nothing

Breathe in
Breathe out
One

Breathe in
Breathe out
Two

Breathe in
Breathe out
Three

I wonder if Sapana's grumpy as she hasn't replied to my
message.

Breathe in
Breathe out
Four

Breathe in
Breathe out

She normally replies within minutes. It's been hours.

Breathe in
Breathe out
Five (or was it six?)

Maybe I should message her.
Maybe I should call.
Maybe I should do it now.

Breathe in
Breathe out
Six

Breathe in
Breathe out
Seven

Breathe in
Breathe out

Why can't I count when I breathe in instead of out?

Breathe in
Breathe out
... **Eight**?

This is so boring. I'm a terrible meditator.

Remember, when your mind wanders,
don't judge yourself for thinking. That's
what minds do.
Just bring it back gently to the breath.
Breathe in, breathe out…

	Breathe in	Breathe in
	Breathe out	Breathe out
Nine	**Ten**	

I must remember to give Alick his pen back.

Breathe in
Breathe out

Maybe I should write that down so I don't forget.

Breathe in
Breathe out

… I have no idea what number I'm on.

Breathe in
Breathe out

One

Laura

The Way

Some snow knows
just where to go
drops straight from sky
to be as one
with other snow

some snow floats
like feathers, lifts
with air and drifts
no rush to get
from high to low

but each and
every downy flake
in silent flight
each one unique
yet dressed in white

can find its way
to gently change
transform with light
by simply settling
to unite

Liz

Everyone

Everyone here is a winner at sport,
scoring goals amid whoops of delight.
Everyone here has expensive new shoes
that are polished – and never too tight.
Everyone here has a house full of books
and reads one in bed every night.

Everyone here has adventurous trips
to places that I've never seen.
Everyone here has gazillions of friends
and brothers who've never been mean.
Everyone here is clever and thin
and their uniform's ironed and clean.

Everyone here has a whopping great house,
with chocolates and sweets guaranteed.
Everyone here lives a life without sad,
a life full of trips to the sea.
Everyone here has a mum and a dad.
Everyone here, except me.

Laura

Consequences

I saw you unfriend Anne
and how you left her in the cold

I saw you say mean things to Anne
I heard the lies you told

I saw you pinching Anne
I saw you tear her books

I saw the others joining in
how scared and sad she looks

I saw you write a nasty note
and put it in her bag

I saw you scare and make Anne sad -
so why do I feel bad?

Liz

Up

Up at the top
of the very big hill
cloud-covered valleys
held everything still.
I knew then and there
that the climb had been
worth it –
and just for a moment
the whole world was

perfect

Matt

In the Heart of a Book

I found myself a story
with a place in me to store it

I found myself a wide, new world
so set off to explore it

I found a scary monster
plus the way to banish it

I found a pool of sadness
and the strength to manage it

I found the dragon in my soul
but learned the way to tame it

I found a new ambition
a path to take and aim it

I found a way to rest my head
while my worries all unplug

I found a curl of comfort
where each word was a hug

I found a web of wonders
things I dream about at night

I found a pair of magic wings
and flew into the light

Liz

First Day

I suffer in science
struggle in maths
eyes on the table
frightened to ask

Mr Mawhinney
face like a goat
must be a hundred
knows I can't cope

Circles the room
stands by my side
speaks to me softly
sparkling eyes

"Here in this school
it's my job to help
I don't want a robot
just be yourself"

Does it so deftly
nobody sees
the rush as my blood
starts to unfreeze

Mr Mawhinney
face like a goat
must be a hundred
brilliant bloke

Matt

Dad's New Girlfriend

"Mum would want me to be happy," he says.
"Mum would want ME to be happy," I say.
     "What I need right now is YOU, Dad," I say.

Except I don't.

Since Mum died, I bury my feelings as deep as they will go.
     And I wonder if Dad will leave me too.

Laura

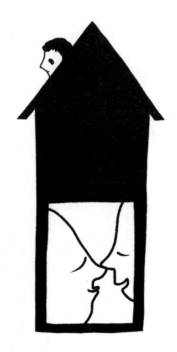

I Don't Forget

I don't forget
to knock, knock, knock
fold and fold
refold my socks
I don't forget
to count to ten
count to ten
and count again
I don't forget
to check the clock
check the clock
and check the lock
put my shoes
in tidy lines
blink three times
blink three times
I don't forget
it gives me faith
this will keep my
family safe

Liz

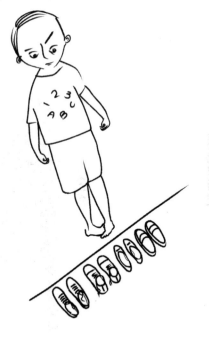

Shame

after we left
in that ice-silent night
I watched my mum become:

a hatcher of plans
weaver of lies
hider of footprints
master of spies

changer of phones
watcher of time
police car avoider
without any crime

worker of jobs
keeper of pride
danger detector
with places to hide

disguiser of past
carrier of blame
protector of dreams
concealer of shame

Matt

Being Heard

When no one
listens

to your
view

your good
ideas

the truth
of you

know they're
the waves

that rise
and crash

all spent
in one

big noisy
splash

you are
the ripple

that rides
inland

and leaves
your tracks

upon the sand

Liz

Full Circle

Every day a little further from the place where I began, every day a little closer being back to who I am.

Matt

Friend

when   I am
empty   but full
of echoes, you find
me, uncrumple me
and cloak me in
kindness
thank
you

.

Laura

About BEING ME

We all have moments when we feel sad, angry or lost, but when we are growing up it is easy to feel alone with our thoughts or feelings. Poems can be a great comfort, as they show us that other people feel and think the same things as we do. No longer are we the only person who feels left out, or worries about being different.

Research tells us that the more chances we get to think and talk about feelings, the easier they are to understand. Talking about thoughts and emotions lets us weave them into a story that makes sense to us. Hearing what other people think can also help us to understand and be kind to other people too. Sometimes, though, we can feel shy or awkward talking about our own feelings. Reading poems can be an easy way to start talking about feelings in general.

The *Being Me* collection beautifully captures a range of emotions that young people often experience. The poems invite reflection and can be used by parents, teachers or other people working with children as a means of opening up sensitive discussion of mental health-related topics.

The following questions can be used for group discussion:
1) How does the poem make you feel?
2) What do you think the main person in the poem is feeling?
3) What does it feel like in your body to have this feeling? For example, does it make your belly hurt? Does it feel heavy?
4) Why do you think the person in the poem feels like this?

5) What could they do to make themselves feel better?
6) What would you say to the person, if they were your friend?

Support

If you are a young person who feels that they need extra support, you could speak with a trusted adult, such as a parent or teacher. If you are a parent/carer with concerns, you can contact your Child's GP for advice.

There are also a number of organisations which provide information and/or further support, including:

Childline: A free confidential service for anyone under 19 https://childline.org.uk

Young Minds: UK charity for children and young people's mental health https://youngminds.org.uk

Support for parents/carers
MindEd for Families: Support for professionals, parents and carers https://mindedforfamilies.org.uk/young-people

NSPCC Children's Mental Health
https://nspcc.org.uk/keeping-children-safe/childrens-mental-health

Dr Karen Goodall, Chartered Psychologist,
University of Edinburgh

About the Poets and Illustrator

Liz Brownlee

Liz is an award-winning poet, editor and film-maker who loves performing and inspiring children and adults at all types of event. Much of her work is about animals, and she is always accompanied by her assistance dog. She is the author, collaborator or editor of six acclaimed books, and is a National Poetry Day Ambassador. She lives in Bristol.

Matt Goodfellow

Matt's first collection for Otter-Barry Books, *Chicken on the Roof*, has become a firm favourite in schools across the UK. His second collection, *Bright Bursts of Colour*, won the poetry section of the North Somerset Book Award. Matt is also the author of the picture book *Shu Lin's Grandpa*, with Yu Rong, and *Caterpillar Cake, Poems to Brighten Your Day*, with Krina Patel Sage, (August 2021), both published by Otter-Barry Books. He lives in Stockport.

Laura Mucha

Laura is an award-winning poet and author. Her debut collection, *Dear Ugly Sisters*, was one of the Independent's Top Ten Poetry Books for Children and BookTrust described it as "stunningly original". Her other books include *Rita's Rabbit* and *We Need to Talk About Love*. Laura has an MA in Psychology and Philosophy and works with organisations such as UNICEF to improve the lives of children.

Victoria Jane Wheeler

Victoria trained at the Royal College of Art. She is a visual artist, illustrator and educator, most often working in art galleries and museums and within higher education. Working to support young people, students and communities, she is passionate about promoting and creating creative opportunities and access to the arts. Her work is held in collections such as Manchester Metropolitan University Special Collections, Preston City Council, and within an educational handling collection at the Whitworth Art Gallery.